A Treasury of Pet Humor

by Oliver Gaspirtz

The Lincoln-Herndon Press
818 South Dirksen Parkway
Springfield, Illinois 62703

A Treasury of Pet Humor

Published by:

The Lincoln-Herndon Press, Inc.
818 South Dirksen Parkway
Springfield, Illinois 62703
(217) 522-2732

Printed in the United States of America.

Library of Congress Cataloguing-in-Publication Data

ISBN 0-942936-36-1

Library of Congress Catalogue Card Number 99-95324
First Edition

Cover and layout by Oliver Gaspirtz.

To Debbie

Don't go in there! It's full of vets!

Top Ten Signs Your Dog Doesn't Like Your Husband

1. Your dog keeps running away, but you always know where to find him: In front of your ex-boyfriend's door.

2. He brings your husband his slippers and he brings you the car keys.

3. He eats a load full of grass in the backyard, comes back in the house and waits by your husband's shoes.

4. When he eats his dogfood, he gags everytime your husband walks past him.

5. After your wedding, your dog played dead for a week.

6. You notice that all the other dogs in the neighborhood keep giving your husband dirty looks.

7. When he's supposed to bring your husband the paper, the only part he brings are the "apartments for rent."

8. When your husband walks the dog, your dog tries to drag him to another neighborhood.

9. When you come home, your dog comes running over to greet you. When your husband comes home, the dog sits down and starts scraping his butt along the carpeted floor.

10. Your husband's cat has been missing for days.

**Stop trying to look so innocent!
Kitty is missing and you're still
burping up furballs.**

A man follows a woman out of a movie theater. She has a dog on a leash. He stops her and says: "I'm sorry to bother you, but I couldn't help but notice that your dog was really into the movie. He cried at the right spots, he moved nervously in his seat at the boring parts, but most of all, he laughed like crazy at the funny parts. Don't you find that unusual?"

"Yes," she replied, "I find it *very* unusual... He hated the book!"

When met by a long procession of people led by a man with a dog, Joe asked the man: "Who died?"

"My Mother in law."

"How?" Joe asked.

"The dog bit her."

"Can I borrow the dog?"

"Get in line."

A man and his dog walk into a bar. The man says, "I'll bet you a round of drinks that my dog can talk." The bartender rolls his eyes and replies: "Yeah! Sure... Go ahead."

So the man asks the dog: "What covers a house?"

And the dog answers: "Roof!"

Then the man asks: "How was your day today?"

And the dog replies: "Rough!"

Finally the man asks: "Who was the greatest ball player of all time?"

Doggy answers: "Ruth!"

The man smiles at the bartender and says: "See? I told you he could talk. Now pay up!"

The bartender throws both of them out the door. Sitting on the sidewalk, the dog looks at his owner and says: "Gehrig?"

A German shepherd went to a Western Union office, took out a blank form and wrote: "Woof, woof, woof, woof, woof, woof, woof, woof, woof."

The clerk examined the paper and said: "There are only nine words here. You could send another 'woof' for the same price."

"But," the dog replied, "that would be silly."

John was excited to finally be asked home to meet the parents of his girlfriend, Betty. Of course he was pretty nervous about the meeting, and by the time John arrived at the doorstep he was in a state of gastric distress.

The problem developed into acute flatulence, and halfway through dinner John just couldn't hold it in one second longer without exploding, so a tiny little fart escaped.

"Rufus!", Betty's mother yelled at the dog lying near John's feet.

Since the dog was getting the blame, John let another, slightly larger one go.

"Rufus!" the mother called out sharply.

"I've got it made," John thought to himself. "One more and I'll feel peachy." So he let loose a thundering big one.

"RUFUS!" shrieked the woman, "Get away from that man before he poops on you!"

◆ ◆ ◆

GASPIRTZ

I Was Framed, I Tell You!

Grizz looks like a mixture between a collie and a German shepherd.

He's the sweetest dog, but when he was younger, you couldn't leave him alone for five minutes!

As soon as no one was looking, he'd use his big wet nose to poke the garbage can until it fell over, tear open the plastic bag inside and go treasure hunting.

Ten minutes later the whole house would look like a battlefield.

He grew out of that habit when he was about 2 years old, but until then there was just no stopping him. All we could do was to hide the garbage can - and all other breakable objects for that matter.

One day my wife and I went to the movies without hiding the garbage can. By the time we realized the oversight, it was already too late. For the remainder of the movie we kept telling each other what horrors to expect once we got home.

Back home, we slowly opened the kitchen door, hoping for the best, but expecting the worst. We were dumbfounded to find the kitchen, the living room, and all other rooms just the way we had left them. We were so proud of Grizz not having wreaked havoc... until we saw him!

There he stood, smiling at us with a picture frame around his neck! Don't ask me how, but somehow he had managed to take a picture off the wall, eat it and stick his head through the frame.

I guess he had been so busy trying to get the frame off of his neck, he just hadn't had time to mess up the rest of the house.

Rosie, the poodle of a wealthy old Jewish widow had died. The heartbroken lady went to her Rabbi and asked, "Rebbe, Rosie is dead. She has been my faithful companion and only friend ever since my Shlomo passed away 9 years ago. Could you please offer a prayer for her?"

The Rabbi replied, "No, I am very sorry, but we cannot hold services for an animal in our synagogue. But not far from here there is a new temple that opened. I heard they're quite liberal over there. Maybe they can hold services for your poodle."

"So I'll go see them now," the old lady said. "Do you think $10,000 will be enough to donate for the service?"

Quickly the Rabbi replied, "So why didn't you tell me Rosie was orthodox?"

A man with a Doberman pinscher and his friend, who owns a chihuahua, are going for a walk. After a while they get hungry and the man with the Doberman pinscher says to his friend: "Let's grab a bite to eat in that restaurant over there!"

The man with the chihuahua replies, "I don't think they'll let us in with our dogs."

"Don't worry about it," the guy with the Doberman pinscher says. He puts on a pair of dark glasses and hands another pair to his friend. Then he tries to walk into the restaurant, but the doorman says: "Sorry, no pets allowed."

The man with the Doberman pinscher says: "You don't understand. This is my seeing-eye dog."

"A Doberman pinscher?" the doorman asks.

"Yes," the man replies, "they're using them now. They're quick learners. I wouldn't know what to do without Rufus."

The doorman nods understandingly and lets the man and his dog pass.

A few minutes later the man with the chihuahua walks over to the restaurant. Again the doorman says: "Sorry, no pets allowed."

The man replies: "But I'm blind. This is my seeing-eye dog."

"A chihuahua?" the doorman wonders.

The man looks surprised and says: "You mean they gave me a chihuahua?"

Top Ten Signs The Veterinarian Likes Your Dog A Little Too Much

1. He relocates his office to be closer to your home.

2. The vet leaves messages for your dog on your answering machine.

3. He throws a surprise party on your dog's birthday.

4. When you had to have your dog spayed, the vet had to seek therapy.

5. On overnight stays, your vet sleeps in the cage with your dog.

6. After having your dog groomed, you notice that the vet has the same haircut.

7. When you come to pick up your dog, the vet tells his receptionist to distract you, so that he can have some time alone with your dog, to say good-bye.

8. He keeps trying to switch your dog with one that looks just like yours.

9. He offers to trade you his 3 kids for your dog.

10. The vet's wife calls you and asks you to tell your dog to leave her husband alone.

Ann woke up one morning and discovered her dog Fluffy was not moving. She brought Fluffy to the vet. After a brief examination, the vet pronounced the dog dead.

"Are you sure?" Ann asked with tears in her eyes. "Isn't there anything else you can do for Fluffy?"

The vet replied, "Well, there is one more thing we could try."

He disappeared in the back room for a second and came back carrying a cat in his arms. He put the cat on the table next to the dog. The cat sniffed the dog from head to toe, jumped off the table and ran back into the other room.

"Well, that confirms it," the vet announced. "Your dog is dead."

"How much do I owe you?" Ann sighed.

"That will be $250," the vet replied.

"What?" Ann yelled. "What did you do that cost $250?"

"Well," the vet replied, "it's $50 for the office visit and $200 for the cat scan."

◆ ◆ ◆

When vets change careers

**You've got to hand it to Adam:
The animals that were going to survive
he gave names like 'cat' and 'dog'. The
ones that didn't he gave names like
'tyrannosaurus' and 'triceratops'.**

A magician was working on a cruise ship in the Caribbean. He had a different audience each week, so he allowed himself to perform the same act over and over again. There was only one problem: The captain's parrot saw the shows each week and began to understand how the magician did every trick.

Once he understood, he started shouting in the middle of every show: "Look, that's not the same hat!"

"Now he's hiding the flowers under the table!"

"Hey, why are all the cards the Ace of Spades?"

The magician was furious but couldn't do anything about it. After all, it was the *captain's* parrot.

One day the unthinkable happened: The ship had an accident and sank! The magician found himself on a piece of wood in the middle of the ocean with the parrot, of course.

They stared at each other with hate, but did not utter a single word. This went on for days.

After a week the parrot finally broke the silence and said: "OK, I give up. Where'd you hide the boat?"

Buster And I Come To Terms

I lived in a duplex where the front doors of each apartment faced each other. My neighbors had just bought an adorable little kitten. He had beautiful long hair and was all white except for two black patches on his head and his tail. Unfortunately my neighbors didn't treat him very well, and the wife bathed him every single day because she didn't like his long hair.

Well, my neighbors had told me that they were moving and wouldn't be able to take the kitten with them. I offered to take him, if they couldn't find a home for him.

When I came home one day, I found my neighbor shoving this cute little three-month-old kitten out the door with his foot. When I openend my door, the kitten ran into my apartment and made a beeline for my daughter's bedroom. I have no idea what the husband did to him, but to this day he doesn't like men too much. He cowers from them until he gets to know them a little better.

My daughter was gone for a few weeks, visiting family. So I decided to close her bedroom door and leave the kitten in there until he got used to the house. Over the next week I tried and tried to make friends with this cat. I can't remember how many times I went into that room, trying to feed him and to coax him out from under my daughter's bed.

He would only come out to eat if I was nowhere near his food. And he growled and hissed the entire time. Every time I tried to pet him, he'd swing his claws at me and hiss. Then he'd quickly run and hide under the bed again. I was really getting frustrated.

Five days later I had had enough: When I walked into the room to feed him, I tried to pet him once again, and when he hissed and swung his claw at me again, that was it! I looked him in the eye and told him that there was no way I was going to have a mean unfriendly cat in my house, and that when I got back from grocery shopping he was gone, gone, gone!

Two hours later I came back from shopping. I put the food in the fridge and decided to give the kitten one last good-bye meal. I walked into my daughter's room with some moist food, a real treat, and called out: "Kitty, kitty, kitty!"

Suddenly he came running out from under the bed and wrapped himself around my ankle like I was his best friend in the whole world. He even let me pet him and purred up a storm. I guess he decided to accept my terms and live with them. He has been my best friend for over nine years now.

Jeana Ridgley of Ridgecrest, CA

Stupid Questions

Q: Why do seagulls fly over the sea?
A: If they flew over the bay they'd be bagels.

Q: What do you call 14 bunnies walking backward?
A: A receding hairline.

Q: Why do birds fly South?
A: Because it's too far to walk.

Q: What is a cat's favorite song?
A: Three Blind Mice.

Q: Why do hummingbirds hum?
A: Because they don't know the words.

Q: What kind of dog tells time?
A: A watch dog.

Q: Why couldn't the pony talk?
A: Because he was a little hoarse.

Q: What time is it when a hippo sits on a chair?
A: Time to get a new chair.

Q: What goes clomp, clomp, clomp, clomp, clomp, clomp, clomp, squoosh?
A: An octopus with one shoe off.

Q: Why do spiders spin webs?
A: Because they can't knit.

Q: What's as big as an elephant but weighs nothing?
A: An elephant's shadow.

Q: What pet can jump higher than a house?
A: All of them. A house can't jump.

Q: What do you get when you cross a tiger with a canary?
A: Who knows, but if it sings, you'd better listen!

The men's room is over there!

Top Ten Signs Your Hamster Doesn't Get Enough Attention

1. He keeps waving and tapping on the glass every time you walk by his cage.

2. He started weaving little baskets out of the woodchip bedding.

3. He made little sculptures out of seeds in his cage.

4. He took up gardening and planted sunflower seeds in the corner of his cage.

5. He has a tiny little imaginary hamster friend.

6. You notice that some of your stuffed animals are missing, and you find them in your hamster's cage.

7. You could swear his sqeaking sounds like the tune to *"I'm so lonesome, I could cry."*

8. You try to figure out how he manages to keep getting away, and you find a tiny book in his cage... *"The Count of Monte Cristo."*

9. He has mold growing on him.

10. You find a tiny little suicide note in his cage.

Irvin based his self-confidence on the theory of relativity.

GASPIRTZ.

A girl was walking down a road near a pond when a toad called: "If you kiss me, I will turn into a handsome prince!"

The girl picked up the toad, smiled at it, and placed it into her backpack.

A few minutes later the toad said: "Look, lady, if you kiss me and turn me back into a handsome prince, I will stay with you for a week."

The girl took the toad out of her backpack, smiled at it, then put it back into the bag.

The toad was starting to get a little restless now: "If you kiss me and turn me back into a handsome prince, I will do anything you want! ANYTHING!"

Again the girl took the toad out of the bag, smiled, and put it back.

Now the toad had had enough: "What is wrong with you? I have told you that I am a handsome prince! And if you kiss me, I will stay with you forever and do ANYTHING you want!"

The girl took the toad out of her backpack again and said: "Look, I am a med student. I have no time for a boyfriend, but a talking toad is cool!"

I've been dreading it, but I think it's time we had a head-to-tail talk about the reproductive process.

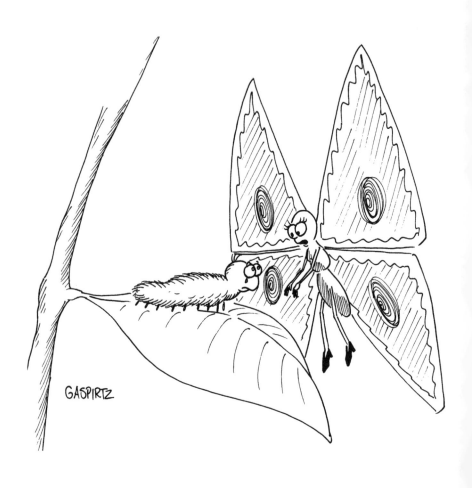

It's not you. It's me. I've changed.

You're suffering from Beetlemania.

Wise Words

"No matter how little money and how few possessions you own, having a pet makes you rich."

Louis Sabin

"The greatest love is a mother's; then a dog's; then a sweetheart's."

Polish Proverb

"A dog teaches a boy fidelity, perseverance, and to turn around three times before lying down."

Robert Benchley

"Did you ever walk into a room and forget why you walked in? I think that is how dogs spend their lives."

Sue Murphy

"Every dog has his day — but the nights are reserved for the cats."

Unknown

"One cat just leads to another."

Ernest Hemingway

"In a cat's eyes, all things belong to cats."

English Proverb

"The problem with cats is that they get the same exact look whether they see a moth or an ax-murderer."

Paula Poundstone

"People who hate cats, will come back as mice in their next life."

Faith Resnick

"When the mouse laughs at the cat there's a hole nearby."

Nigerian Proverb

If dogs could read

Chef's Ice-Capades

A few years ago my wife and I went on a trip to Berlin. It was the middle of Winter. We decided to go for a walk with our two dogs, Boss and Chef, and enjoy the crisp cold air.

As we passed a small lake, Chef, a spunky schnauzer, ran out onto the frozen surface. We tried to stop him, but he wouldn't listen. Slipping and sliding, he ran across the ice.

All of a sudden he noticed that there was water under his feet. Somehow he must have realized that he was in danger of falling through the thin layer of ice, because suddenly he stopped dead in his tracks.

His legs were shaking and his whole body was shivering in fear.

We kept calling him, but he just stood there, frozen. He was too scared to walk back off the ice. He was petrified. I figured, maybe

he'd feel safer, If I threw a blanket out onto the lake. He wouldn't see the water that way. It didn't help. Chef just stood there, looking at us with his big brown eyes.

After a couple of minutes we found a log nearby. I gently eased it onto the ice, hoping Chef would feel safe enough on the log to get back on land. No luck.

Finally I realized that I had no other choice but to go get him. I took off my pants and my wintercoat, and walked towards Chef. The ice on top of the painfully cold water was not strong enough to support my weight, so I had to wade through the water while the edge of the icy surface kept scraping my thighs and the rocks at the bottom of the lake kept cutting my bare feet.

Chef was terrified! And for every inch I got closer to him, he walked further out into the middle of the lake. Just a few more feet and the water was going to be too deep to walk. Luckily I was able to grab him before one of us drowned... But I don't think I have to tell you how embarrassed I was, standing there in my bloomers, soaking wet and freezing.

Hermann Westhoff of Aachen, Germany

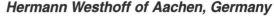

How kittens learn to land on all four paws.

More Stupid Questions

Q: Why is Stevie Wonder's right leg yellow?
A: Because his dog is blind, too.

Q: Where do you find a turtle with no legs?
A: Where ever you left it.

Q: What's black and white, black and white, black and white, and black and white?
A: A penguin rolling down a hill.

Q: What's six feet long and hangs from trees in Africa?
A: Elephant snot.

Q: Why do ostriches have such long legs?
A: So their feet will touch the ground.

Q: What do you call a five-day-old dog in Switzerland?
A: A puppy.

Q: What do you call a cat with a machine gun?
A: Sir.

Q: What does a snail do on a tortoise's back?
A: "Vrooom... vrooom... vrooooooom..."

Q: How do you know if there is an elephant under the bed?
A: Your nose is touching the ceiling.

Q: Why did the cat cross the road?
A: Chicken's day off.

Q: Why did the fish get turned down by the Army?
A: He failed his herring test.

Q: What do you get when you cross a parrot with a centipede?
A: A walkie-talkie.

Peek-A-Boo!

Spanky & Tammy

Roy was a gas station attendant. One day he was filling up another car, when he spotted three penguins sitting on the back seat of the car. Baffled, Roy asked the driver: "What's up with those penguins?"

The man in the car replied: "I found them by the side of the road. But to tell you the truth, I have no idea what to do with them."

Roy wasn't the sharpest knife in the drawer, but after a few minutes of hard thinking he came up with a pretty good idea: "You should take them to the zoo," he said.

"Great idea," the man in the car smiled and drove away.

The next day the man with the car was back at Roy's gas station. And the penguins were still in the back seat of the car!

"Hey, they're still here! I thought you were going to take them to the zoo," Roy said.

"Oh, I did," said the driver, "and we had a great time! Today I'm taking them to the beach."

On her way to work a lady passed a new pet shop. She had a few minutes to spare, so she walked into the store and took a look around. Near the store window she saw a cage with a beautiful red parrot in it. She admired him for a few minutes, when the parrot said to her: "Hey lady, you are really ugly!"

A little upset at the rude parrot, the woman left the store and went to work.

Later that day on her way home from the office she saw the same parrot in the window. Again the parrot squawked: "Hey lady, you are really ugly!"

Mad at the bird, she rushed home.

When she passed the pet store on her way to work the next morning, the parrot said it again: "Hey lady, you are really ugly!"

Well, the lady was furious! Cursing in a rather unlady-like manner, she stormed into the store and demanded to see the owner. She told him that she was going to sue him and kill the bird if he didn't stop harassing her. The man behind the counter apologized and promised the bird would not say it again.

When the lady walked past the store after work the parrot squawked: "Hey lady..."

She paused and said, "Yes?"

And the bird said: "You know."

38

Ben and Jake, two college students, bought a parrot from a pet shop. The parrot was highly intelligent, but all he ever did was swear. He had an amazing vocabulary. He could swear for five minutes straight without repeating himself. At first the two room mates thought it was the coolest bird ever, but after days and nights of constant verbal abuse and obscenities, even the students couldn't take it anymore.

"Dude, we're gonna have to teach that bird a lesson," Ben said.

He grabbed the parrot by the neck and stuck him in the refrigerator. "That'll cool him off a bit!"

For the first few seconds all hell seemed to break loose. The bird kicked and clawed and thrashed. Then suddenly everything was very quiet.

The two students started to worry that the bird might be hurt, so Jake opened the fridge.

The parrot calmly climbed onto Jake's outstretched arm and said in a very polite manner: "Awfully sorry about the trouble I gave you. I'll do my best to improve my vocabulary from now on."

Ben and Jake were totally amazed. They couldn't understand the transformation that had come over the parrot.

After a few minutes the parrot asked: "By the way, what did the chicken do?"

◆ ◆ ◆

Paranoid Parrot

About 4 years ago I was caught in a hen house, so I claimed to be a vet. Then it was either keep up the act or get skinned. So I picked the option that paid $60,000 a year.

**Quick, get the antidote!
Roger bit his tongue again!**

Pet Trivia

In 1888, 300,000 mummies of cats were found at Beni Hassan, Egypt. They were sold at about $18 per ton and shipped to England, where the mummified pets were ground up and used as fertilizer.

A bird requires more food in proportion to its size than a baby or a cat.

Goldfish lose their color if they are kept in dim light or are placed in a body of running water, such as a stream.

Cats have over one hundred vocal sounds, while dogs only have about ten.

Every year, $1.5 billion is spent on pet food. This is four times the amount spent on baby food.

An iguana can stay under water for 28 minutes.

German Shepherds bite humans more than any other breed of dog.

All pet hamsters are descended from a single female wild golden hamster found with a litter of 12 young in Syria in 1930.

A chameleon's tongue is twice the length of its body.

A rat can last longer without water than a camel can.

Certain frogs can be frozen solid, then thawed, and continue living.

A cat has 32 muscles in each ear.

By feeding hens certain dyes they can be made to lay eggs with varicolored yolks.

A cat's jaws cannot move sideways.

According to ancient Greek literature, when Odysseus arrived home after an absence of 20 years, disguised as a beggar, the only one to recognize him was his aged dog Argos, who wagged his tail at his master, and then died.

Sure, liposuction has its risks, but around here it has added years to my life.

Sleeping Beauties

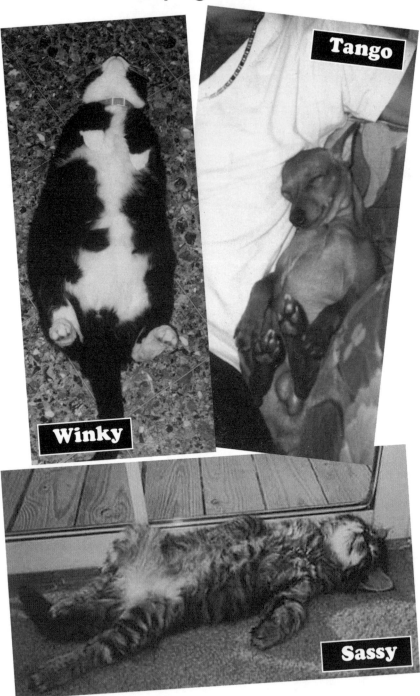

The New English-Dogish Dictionary

Top Ten Things To Do During Pet Appreciation Week

1. Lick your dog's face.

2. Get your dog a bone and bury it for him.

3. Mark your territory by peeing on the couch.

4. Bring your cat a dead bird.

5. Make a real effort to learn to purr.

6. Spend a day with your head stuck in a bird cage.

7. Spend quality time with your pet rolling around in something really awful.

8. Sniff your neighbor's butt.

9. Bite the mailman.

10. Eat supper on the floor.

GASPIRTZ

A-ha! I thought I smelled doggie breath when you kissed me!

I'll have the premium homestyle chunks in kibbles sauce, with chicken, cheese bits and bacon.

**The new trend among bank robbers:
pitbull hold-ups**

A robber broke into the house of a family just after they had left to go to church one evening. He was rummaging through the upstairs rooms when he heard a voice saying: "Jesus is watching you!"

Fearing the family might have come home early, he snuck downstairs. When he didn't see anyone, he continued looking for valuables. Plundering the silver cabinet, he heard the voice again. This time from right behind him: "Jesus is watching you!"

He threw his arms in the air and turned around with his heart pounding. But there was no one there... Except for a little green parrot in a birdcage.

Relieved, the robber chuckled and said : "Hey, birdie! Let me guess! Your name is Jesus."

"Bwak... No," said the bird, "my name is Moses."

"Moses!?!" the robber wondered. "What kind of weirdos name their bird Moses?"

"Bwak... The same weirdos that named their pitbull 'Jesus'."

What's brown and black and looks good on a lawyer?
A pitbull.

Did you hear about the new dog breed in pet shops?
They crossed a pitbull with a collie. First it bites your leg off and then it goes for help.

What has four legs and an arm?
A happy pitbull.

What's the difference between a female lawyer and a pitbull?
Lipstick!

Enjoying An Afternoon Treat

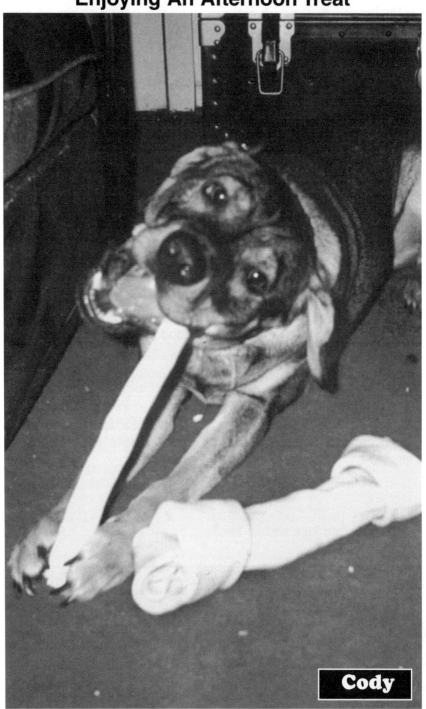

Cody

**He won't talk.
He used to be in the mob.**

Lately you've been cold to me, Frank.

Somehow, running aimlessly in circles, barking at harmless passersby, and destroying the evening paper have become meaningless.

Pet Trivia

Which is the only domestic animal not mentioned in the Bible?
The cat.

Did you know that no two spider webs are ever the same?

Why do owls turn their heads in that strange manner?
They can't move their eyes, because their eyeballs are not round like ours, but tubular.

Did you know that pet parrots can eat virtually any common human food, except for chocolate and avocados? Those are highly toxic to a parrot and can be fatal.

Which animals can get sunburns like humans?
Pigs, walruses, and light-colored horses.

Rats are omnivorous. They do not only eat almost any type of food, but even dead or dying members of their own species.

When was the ASPCA formed?
In 1866.

Did you know there are about 2,600 different species of frogs? They live on every continent, except Antarctica.

The bloodhound is the only animal whose evidence is admissible in an American court.

Which is the only bird that can fly backwards?
The hummingbird.

The bones of a pigeon weigh less than its feathers.

Which was the largest animal ever seen alive?
A female blue whale. She was 113.5 foot long and weighed about 170 tons.

A male kangaroo is called a boomer. A female kangaroo is called a doe or a flyer. A baby kangaroo is called a joey.

You just *WHAT?!*

Oh, good! You and Fido are getting aquainted. Isn't he adorable?

Top Ten Signs You Spoil Your Dog

1. You think begging for table scraps is beneath him, so you let your dog eat at the table with you.

2. You take him to the supermarket and let him pick out his own dog food.

3. Your husband comes home from work, looks at the stew on the stove and asks: "Is this people food or dog food?"

4. You bought matching His & Hers place mats for your dog and yourself.

5. At dinner parties you always have to double-check the butter for visible lick marks, before putting it on the table.

6. Your dog gets to vote on where to spend the next family vacation.

7. You don't care if you or your spouse are comforable at night, as long as Fido has enough room on the bed.

8. You complain about the rising costs of groceries, but you don't think twice about spending a fortune on doggie treats.

9. Your dog always gets the best spot on the couch and sometimes he even gets to hold the remote.

10. He has his own e-mail address.

Sure, he *watches* Masterpiece Theatre, but he doesn't *get* it.

Why dogs never get any good jobs.

And this is our deluxe model, complete with jacuzzi.

How long are you in for?

There goes the neighborhood!

Hasso The Amazing Cat Catcher

They say cats and dogs don't get along. Well, Hasso proved them wrong! Hasso was the sweetest and gentlest German shepherd I have ever seen.

A couple of years ago we had a cat named Susie. She gave birth to a litter of 6 or 7 kittens. When the kittens got into trouble, Susie would grab them by the neck and carry them back into her basket. Hasso watched and learned.

As the kittens grew up, Hasso watched over them like a daddy. And if he'd catch them scratch the side of the couch or sneak into a room they weren't allowed in, he'd gently grab them by the neck and carry them back to their basket.

And the most amazing part was that our cats let him do it! They weren't afraid of him and they never got mad. They'd just hold still until he let go of them. He actually got so good at it that we could tell him "Go, get kitty!" and he'd run and bring us the nearest cat.

No, we will not grant maternity leave just because your cat had five kittens.

Top Ten Warning Signs That You Are A "Crazy Cat Lady"

1. Your colleagues no longer ask how your weekend was. Instead they ask how your cats are doing.

2. People at work have stopped offering you their lint brushes. They realize it's hopeless anyway.

3. When you get your latest roll of film developed, there's not a single human being in the pictures.

4. You have more cats than the local pet store and there are several kitty litter boxes in every room of your apartment.

5. Your personal motto is: "You can never have enough cats."

6. You buy more than 60 pounds of cat litter a month.

7. You'd rather watch hours of boring infomercials than disturb the cat sleeping on the remote.

8. You choose your friends based on how well your cats like them.

9. The only time you leave your apartment is to feed the stray cats in the neighborhood.

10. You introduce your cats by name to the pizza delivery guy.

**Can't I leave you two alone
for five minutes?**

Happy Birthday!

Cory

Creepy Crawlers

There are more insects in one square mile of rural land than there are human beings on the entire earth.

Which is the world's smallest mammal?
The bumblebee bat of Thailand. It weighs less than a penny.

Everyone knows the blood of mammals is red and the blood of insects is usually yellow. But what color is the blood of lobsters?
Blue.

Which animal is responsible for the most human deaths worldwide?
The mosquito.

Experts say you're more likely to get bit by mosquitoes if you eat bananas.

A cockroach can live a week without its head. The roach only dies because without a mouth, it can't drink water and dies of thirst.

Did you know that some female cockroaches mate once and are pregnant for the rest of their lives?

Cockroaches can swim, but coming up for air is difficult since they breathe through their sides, not their noses or mouths. But that is not much of a problem since a cockroach can hold its breath for about 40 minutes.

The venom of a female black widow spider is more potent than that of a rattlesnake.

The poison-arrow frog has enough poison to kill about 2,200 people.

Did you know that the poisonous copperhead snake smells like fresh cut cucumbers?

By the way, snakes are immune to their own poison.

The honey bee kills more people worldwide than all the poisonous snakes combined.

GASPIRTZ

A lesser known relative of the Killer Bee: The Hara-Kiri Bee

A guy was stranded on a lonely island with only a pitbull and a pig for company. There was plenty of food and fresh water, so he was doing alright for a few months. But eventually the loneliness got to him... If you know what I mean.

The pig started to look more and more attractive - soft, pink skin, round buttocks, etc. But every time this poor guy tried to make an advance towards the pig, the pitbull growled at him. Once he almost got bit. The guy was getting very frustrated.

One day a life raft washed ashore. In it was a beautiful unconscious woman. The guy carried her back to his hut and nursed her back to health. After a few days the woman regained her strength and said: "Thank you, thank you so much for saving my life! I don't know how I can ever repay you. I'll do anything for you, anything you want!"

The guy thought for a moment and said, "Would you mind taking my dog for a walk?"

Knowing that Aunt Jane had left all her money to her cat, Harvey came prepared.

**Once upon a time there were three
little pigs, so I ate them. End of story.
Now go to sleep.**

About Dogs...

"Whoever said you can't buy happiness forgot about puppies."
Gene Hill

"There is no psychiatrist in the world like a puppy licking your face."
Ben Williams

"The average dog is a nicer person than the average person."
Andrew A. Rooney

"A dog is the only thing on earth that loves you more than he loves himself."
Josh Billings

"Don't accept your dog's admiration as conclusive evidence that you are wonderful."
Ann Landers

"In order to keep a true perspective of one's importance, everyone should have a dog that will worship him and a cat that will ignore him."
Dereke Bruce

"Cat's Motto: No matter what you've done wrong, always try to make it look like the dog did it."
Unknown

"Some days you're the dog, some days you're the hydrant."
Unknown

"I wonder if other dogs think poodles are members of a weird religious cult."
Rita Rudner

"If your dog is fat, you aren't getting enough exercise."
Unknown

"I wonder what goes through his mind when he sees us peeing in his water bowl."
Penny Ward Moser

**I wish he would just bury
his bones without the fuss.**

When you told me you wanted a toy dog, I expected it to run on batteries.

He's afraid of heights.

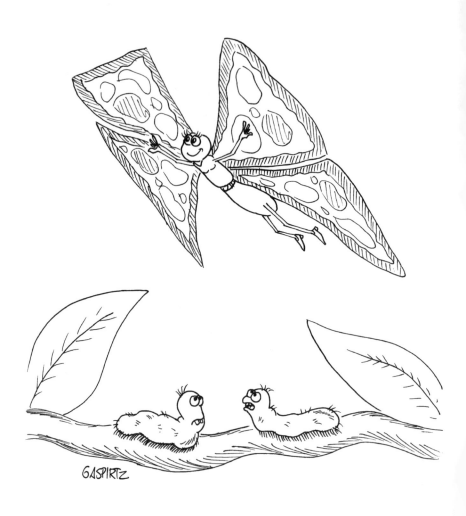

**Well, Gloria has certainly come
out of her shell.**

A farmer sent his nephew a crate of chickens, but the box burst open just as the boy started to take them out. The next day he wrote his uncle, "I chased them through my neighbor's yard, but only got back eleven."

The uncle wrote back: "You did all right. I only sent six."

Two bats were sitting in a cave. Suddenly one flew out into the night and yelled: "Man, I'm starving! I need to get some blood!"

He returned about three hours later, with blood dripping from his fangs and mouth.

"Where'd you get the blood from?" asked the other bat.

"Well, you go out the cave... And you see the first tree on the left?"

"Yes," the other bat replied.

"Well, I didn't."

"What's wrong with your husband?" the psychiatrist asked.

"He thinks he's a chicken," answered the woman.

"How long has he been acting like a chicken?"

"Three years. We would have come in sooner, but we needed the eggs."

A priest went to buy a parrot.

"Are you sure it doesn't swear?" asked the priest.

"Oh absolutely. It's a religious parrot," the storekeeper assured him.

"Do you see those strings on his legs? When you pull the right one, he recites the lord's prayer, and when you pull on the left, he recites the 23rd Psalm."

"Wonderful!" said the priest, "but what happens if you pull both strings?"

"I'll fall off my friggin' perch, you idiot!" screeched the parrot.

A mother and her son were walking down the road.

Suddenly she said: "Look, Johnny, that's a puddle of H2O."

"No," said Johnny, "that's a puddle of K9P."

More Stupid Questions

Q: What do you get when you cross a fly with an elephant?
A: A zipper that never forgets.

Q: Where does virgin wool come from?
A: Ugly sheep.

Q: How do you tell when a moth farts?
A: It flies in a straight line.

Q: What would you get if Batman and Robin were run over by a herd of stampeding elephants?
A: Flatman and Ribbon.

Q: What do you call a woodpecker with no beak?
A: A headbanger.

Q: Why can't Smokey the Bear's wife get pregnant?
A: Every time she gets hot, he beats her out with a shovel.

Q: What did the Cinderella fish wear to the ball?
A: Glass flippers.

Q: What is green and pecks on trees?
A: Woody Wood Pickle.

Q: How do you catch a runaway dog?
A: Hide behind a tree and make a noise like a bone!

Q: Why is an elephant gray, large and wrinkled?
A: Because if it were small, round, and white, it would be an aspirin.

Q: What did the cat who had no money say?
A: I'm paw.

Q: What do you get if you cross an alley cat with a Chinese cat?
A: A Peking Tom.

Q: What happened to the cat that swallowed a ball of wool?
A: She had mittens.

I only tolerate them for the food.

On Top Of The World

Oscar

Noel

I just hope Kitty won't bring me a dead mouse again.

"You enter into a certain amount of madness when you marry a person with pets."

Nora Ephron

"Women and cats will do as they please, and men and dogs should relax and get used to the idea."

Robert A. Heinlein

Moon!

Rex

Top Ten Reasons Why
It's Great To Be A Dog

1. If it itches, you can reach it. And no matter where it itches, no one will be offended if you scratch it in public.

2. No one notices if you have hair growing in weird places as you get older.

3. Personal hygiene is a blast: No one expects you to take a bath every day, and you don't even have to comb your own hair.

4. Having a wet nose is considered a sign of good health.

5. No one thinks less of you for passing gas. Some people might actually think you're cute.

6. Who needs a big home entertainment system? A bone or an old shoe can entertain you for hours.

7. You can spend hours just smelling stuff.

8. No one ever expects you to pay for lunch or dinner. You never have to worry about table manners, and if you gain weight, it's someone else's fault.

9. It doesn't take much to make you happy. You're always excited to see the same old people. All they have to do is leave the room for five minutes and come back.

10. Every garbage can looks like a cold buffet to you.

Alright! Alright! I'll talk!

I'm gonna be a wheel someday.

Jim decided he wanted to get an exotic pet. So he walked into a nearby pet store to buy a parrot. The shop owner pointed to three very similar looking birds on a perch and explained: "The parrot on the left costs 500 dollars."

"Wow! That's a lot of money," Jim said, "Why is it so expensive?" The store owner replied: "Well, this particular breed is extremely intelligent. This bird actually knows how to use a computer!"

Jim was amazed and asked about the next parrot. The owner told him that one cost 1,000 dollars, because it could not only use a computer but it even knew how to program software.

Increasingly startled, Jim asked about the third parrot. The store owner told him that it cost 2,000 dollars.

"Unbelievable!", Jim exclaimed, "What can it do?"

The owner replied: "To be honest, I have never actually seen it do a thing, but the other two call him boss."

An old lady was rocking away the last of her days on her front porch, petting the cat on her lap, reflecting on her long life, when all of a sudden a fairy godmother appeared in front of her.

"You have won the fairy godmother lottery! Congratulations! You have three wishes!" the fairy godmother said.

"Oh, my!" the old lady exclaimed. "I guess I would like to be really rich."

POOF!

The fairy godmother snapped her fingers and the old lady's little house was suddenly a huge Victorian mansion.

"And I guess I wouldn't mind being a young, beautiful princess."
POOF!

Suddenly the old lady was a breathtakingly beautiful young woman.

Then the lady looked at the cat on her lap, who had been her best friend and only companion for many years, and said: "Can you change him into a handsome prince?"

POOF!

Suddenly an unbelievably handsome young man stood in front of her.

She stared at him, lovestruck. With a smile that made her heart melt, he leaned over to her, and whispered in her ear: "I bet you're sorry you had me neutered."

More About Dogs...

"Money will buy you a pretty good dog, but it won't buy the wag of his tail."

Unknown

"Dogs are our link to paradise. They don't know evil or jealousy or discontent. To sit with a dog on a hillside on a glorious afternoon is to be back in Eden, where doing nothing was not boring, it was peace."

Milan Kundera

"If you pick up a starving dog and make him prosperous, he will not bite you; that is the principal difference between a dog and a man."

Mark Twain

"Histories are more full of examples of the fidelity of dogs than of friends."

Alexander Pope

"He is your friend, your partner, your defender, your dog. You are his life, his love, his leader. He will be yours, faithful and true, to the last beat of his heart. You owe it to him to be worthy of such devotion."

Unknown

"When you leave them in the morning, they stick their nose in the door crack and stand there like a portrait until you turn the key eight hours later."

Erma Bombeck

"Ever consider what they must think of us? I mean, here we come back from a grocery store with the most amazing haul: chicken, pork, half a cow. They must think we're the greatest hunters on earth!"

Anne Tyler

"Outside of a dog, a book is probably man's best friend; inside of a dog, it's too dark to read."

Groucho Marx

"When a man's best friend is his dog, that dog has a problem."

Edward Abbey

"I loathe people who keep dogs. They are cowards who haven't got the guts to bite people themselves."

August Strindberg

**I have kids, and this bird repeats
every word my husband says.**

Big deal. Dogs are pack animals.

Top Ten Reasons Why Dogs Are Better Pets Than Cats

1. Dogs will tilt their heads and try to understand every word you say. Cats will ignore you and take a nap.

2. Cats look silly on a leash.

3. When you come home from work, your dog will be happy and lick your face. Cats will still be mad at you for leaving in the first place.

4. Dogs will give you unconditional love until the day they die. Cats will make you pay for every mistake you've ever made since the day you were born.

5. A dog knows when you're sad. And he'll try to comfort you. Cats don't care how you feel, as long as you remember where the can-opener is.

6. Dogs will bring you your slippers.
   Cats will drop a dead mouse in your slippers.

7. When you take them for a ride, dogs will sit on the seat next to you. Cats have to have their own private basket, or they won't go at all.

8. Dogs will come when you call them. And they'll be happy. Cats will have someone take a message and get back to you.

9. Dogs will play fetch with you all day long. The only thing cats will play with all day long are small rodents or bugs, preferably ones that look like they're in pain.

10. Dogs will wake you up if the house is on fire.
    Cats will quietly sneak out the back door.

**This of course is Mittens.
And this one is a picture
of my husband John.**

Things You Should Know About Cats

Cats have the simplest of taste - the best will suffice.

Dogs are like kids. Cats are like roommates.

Cats are living proof that eating and sleeping all day isn't all bad.

Cats teach us that not everything in nature has a function.

Traits we despise in people, we prize as virtues in cats.

Cats know all the sunny places.

An aquarium is just interactive television for cats.

A cat's favorite game is: "Hah! Made you look!"

A cat's worst enemy is a closed door.

Cats aren't clean, they're just covered with cat spit.

Cats aren't as dignified as people say they are. Ever watched a cat clean its privates?

Cats are good for dusting high places.

Cats have fur coats because they look silly in raincoats.

You don't own your cat. The cat owns you. And the cat owns the house. You just pay the mortgage.

Cats have their own lives; get on with yours.

Someone once said: "He who doesn't like cats doesn't like pets smarter than he." But cats aren't that intelligent. They just THINK they are.

Men don't like cats because cats are cooler than they are.

Cats aren't so brave anymore once they're in a microwave.

Snapshots!

Whiskey

Barney

George and Barney

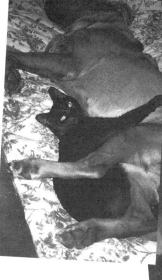

Alli

Maddie

**Don't worry, he doesn't bite.
But when he drools it can get
dangerous.**

GASPIRTZ

A guy was helping a farmer get a load of hay out from the barn when he noticed a pig with a wooden leg limping around in front of the barn. So he asked the farmer: "Did you see that pig? What's with the wooden leg?"

The farmer sat down on a bale of hay and began to tell the guy the pig's story:

"One day," he began, "my wife and I were sleeping upstairs, when the pig came running in, jumped into our bed with us, and squealed like mad. So we got up and went outside to see what was going on. The old stove down in the kitchen had exploded. The flames were everywhere. The whole house was on fire! If it hadn't been for that pig, my wife and I wouldn't be alive today."

"Wow! That's amazing!" the guy said. "So the pig lost that leg in the fire?"

"Well no," replied the farmer. "One day when I was plowing the field out back, my tractor tipped over and I was trapped underneath and couldn't free myself. That same pig came over, dug me out and saved my life!"

"Incredible!" said the guy. "But how did that pig lose his leg?"

"Well, a great pig like that, we ain't gonna eat all at once!"

GASPIRTZ

**He's been burying bones all afternoon,
ever since he saw that TV-show about
the Y2K bug.**

GASPIRTZ

**Yes, they had me fixed and declawed.
But I figure that living well is the best
revenge.**

100

A customer in a little country drug store noticed a sign with the words "Danger! Beware of Dog!" written on it. But instead of a well-trained watch dog, all he saw was a harmless old hound dog sleeping on the floor next to the cash register.

He asked the owner of the store: "Is THAT the dog people are supposed to beware of?!"

"Yessiree, that's him," the owner replied.

The customer couldn't help but laugh. "That sure doesn't look like a dangerous dog to me. Why on Earth would you post that sign?"

"Because until I hung up that sign, folks kept tripping over him."

Three successful Jewish brothers compared their wealth by the presents they had recently sent their old mother for her 75th birthday.

Shlomo, the oldest, said: "I built a big mansion for our mother."

Moishe, the second, said: "I sent her a Mercedes with a driver."

Ira, the youngest, said: "You remember how our mama used to enjoy reading the bible? Now she can't see very well. So I sent her a remarkable parrot that recites the whole bible... Mama just has to name the chapter and verse."

A few days later a letter arrived from their mother.

"Shlomo," she wrote, "the mansion you built is so huge. I live only in one room, but I have to clean the whole house."

"Moishe," she wrote, "I am too old to travel. I stay most of the time at home so I rarely use the Mercedes. And that driver - he's a pain in the tuchas."

"But Ira," she wrote, "the chicken was delicious!"

A bear and a rabbit were taking a dump in the woods. The bear looked over to the rabbit and asked: "Mr. Rabbit, do you ever have a problem with poop sticking to your fur?"

The rabbit replied: "Why no, Mr. Bear, I most certainly do not."

So the bear wiped his butt with the rabbit.

Cindy: "I've lost my cat!"
Rose: "Why don't you put an ad in the newspaper?"
Cindy: "Don't be silly! She can't read."

I Always Get The Blame!

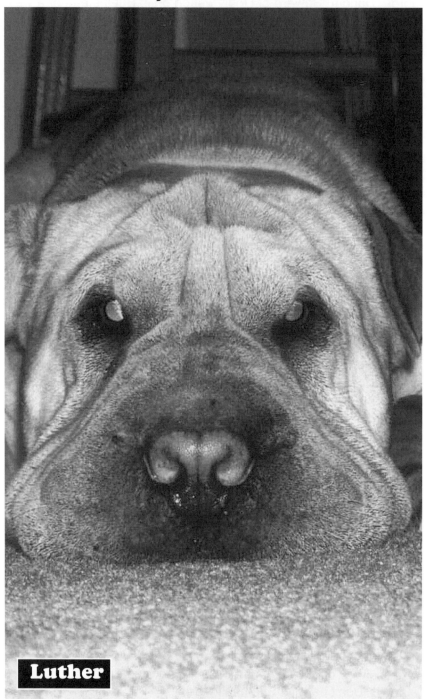

Luther

**Gerbils are OK. So are snakes.
But not BOTH!**

One Sunday morning John stepped out onto the porch in his bathrobe to pick up his newspaper. He noticed a snail on the paper, so he picked it up and flung it across the front lawn onto the sidewalk.

On another Sunday morning, about two years later, John was out on the porch again to pick up his paper, when he noticed a snail on the paper.

It was the same snail.

Bill looked at the snail. The snail looked at Bill.

Then the snail said: "Now, was that REALLY necessary?!"

Ricky, Jimmy, and Stewy were on the bus home from elementary school, when a fire engine zoomed past their bus with blaring sirens.

The three kids noticed a Dalmatian dog on the front seat of the fire engine, and Ricky said: "They use that dog to keep crowds back."

"No," said Jimmy, "he's just for good luck."

But Stewy knew better: "No, the dog is giving them directions to the nearest fire hydrant."

After a long day at the office, Chris came home one day to find his dog with the neighbor's pet rabbit in his mouth.

The rabbit was obviously dead. Chris panicked!

"If my neighbors find out my dog killed their bunny, they'll hate me forever," he thought.

So he took the dirty, chewed up rabbit into the house, gave it a bath and blow-dried its fur.

Chris knew his neighbors kept their backdoor open during the summer, so he snuck inside and put the bunny back into the cage, hoping his neighbors would think it died of natural causes.

A couple of days later Chris and his neighbor saw each other outside.

"Did you hear that Fluffy died?" the neighbor asked.

"Oh. Uhmm... Sorry to hear that. What happened?" Chris mumbled.

The neighbor replied: "We just found him dead in his cage one day. But the strange thing is that the day after we buried him, we went out to dinner and someone must have dug him up, gave him a bath and put him back into the cage! There are some really sick people out there!"

I'd say either he needs a girlfriend
or he has a hell of a case of
separation anxiety.

I think this is all a big conspiracy and the purpose of that wheel is to keep us slim enough to be flushable.

John Smith noticed a parrot sitting on the seat next to him in business class. When the stewardess came by, the parrot nastily yelled: "Hey, bimbo! Bring me a Vodka and tonic! And make it snappy!"

The startled stewardess then looked at Mr. Smith and asked him what he wanted to drink. John asked her to bring him a Scotch and water. A few minutes later the stewardess returned with the Vodka and tonic for the parrot, but nothing for John.

After the nasty parrot finished his drink, he arrogantly demanded another Vodka and tonic. John politely reminded the stewardess that he was still waiting for the Scotch he had ordered. When the stewardess returned, she had the Vodka and tonic for the parrot, but again did not bring anything for John.

Now John started to get upset at the stewardess for ignoring him in favor of the rude parrot. So the next time she approached his seat, John yelled: "Hey, bitch! Get me my drink! NOW!"

Immediately two male flight attendants showed up, grabbed both John and the parrot, dragged them to the door and threw them off the plane in mid-air. As they were falling to the ground, the parrot looked at John and said: "You sure got guts for someone who can't fly."

Sorry, but we won't break up the set.

I'm afraid the years of drug-sniffing have resulted in a permanent state of euphoria.

One day a cat died and went to Heaven. There she met The Lord Himself. God said to the cat: "You lived a good life and if there is anything I can do to make your stay in Heaven more comfortable, please, don't hesitate to let Me know."

After a moment of thought, the cat replied: "Lord, all my life I have lived with a poor family and had to sleep on a hard wooden floor. Just once would I like to have a nice soft pillow to call my own."

The Lord smiled, and a beautiful velvet pillow appeared out of nowhere.

A few days later eight farm mice were killed in an accident and went to Heaven. They, too, were greeted by God Himself with the same question. The mice answered: "All of our lives we've been chased by cats, dogs, and even by women with brooms. We never want to have to run again. Do you think we could have inline skates? They look like a lot of fun."

Suddenly all of them wore tiny inline skates with colorful little wheels.

About a week or so later, God visited the cat to see how she was doing.

Rolled up in a ball, she was laying on her pillow, sleeping. God gently woke her up and asked: "So, how do you like it up here?"

The cat stretched and yawned: "It is wonderful here! I love what you've done with the place. And great service! Those Meals On Wheels you've been sending me were a nice touch!"

I need a pet that fits my husband's
personality. Got any sloths?

What dogs hear

Snakey can sense when someone doesn't like him, dad.

A snail was going along the beach when he happened to look back behind him and saw three turtles wearing leather jackets. After going on for about four weeks, the snail looked back again and saw that the three turtles were still there and closing in on him. So the snail picked up his pace. After about six more weeks, the snail looked back again, and saw that the turtles were still chasing him. And they were getting closer and closer! So he kept on going as fast as he could. After another few weeks the turtles finally caught up with the snail and mugged him, took all of his clothes and the keys to his car. After another couple of weeks the snail got to a pay phone and called the police.

"I've been mugged by three turtles wearing leather jackets! You need to get down here and take a report or do something," he said.

"Can you give us a description of the turtles?" asked the police officer.

"No, I can't. It all happened too fast!" cried the snail.

Bob was in love with Nancy, the beautiful young woman across the street. Unfortunately Bob had a speech impediment and she wouldn't marry him because he talked funny. One day he read about a school on the other side of the country, that might be able to help him overcome his handicap. So he enrolled for four months.

When Bob returned, his buddy Jimmy picked him up at the airport and asked: "So? Was it worth it? Were they able to help you?"

Bob replied: "Well - sort - of. - But - now - I - must - talk - very - slow - and - be - very - careful - to - articulate - words - properly."

Jimmy smiled and said: "Don't worry! Nancy loves you. I'm sure she'll marry you."

Later that night Jimmy dropped Bob off at Nancy's house. But about two hours later Bob rang Jimmy's doorbell.

Jimmy asked: "What are you doing here? Does that mean she's not going to marry you after all?"

Bob answered: "No, - I - don't - think - so."

"Why? What happened?" Jimmy asked.

Bob explained: "Well, - everything - went - well - at - first. - We - were - sitting - on - the - couch - talking - and - I - saw - the - cat - playing - with - the - balls - on - the - Christmas - tree, - so - I - tried - to - be - witty - and - said: "Look, - honey, - after - we're - married, - you - can - do - that - to - me!" - But - by - the - time - I - said - it - and - she - looked, - the - cat - was - licking - his - butt!"

Mrs. Lonefold's dishwasher quit working, so she decided to call a repairman. He couldn't accommodate her with an evening appointment, and since she had to go to work the next day, she told him: "I'll leave the key under the mat. Fix the dishwasher, leave the bill on the counter, and I'll mail you the check. By the way, don't worry about my Rottweiler. He won't bother you. But whatever you do, do NOT talk to my parrot!"

When the repairman arrived at Mrs. Lonefold's apartment the next day, he discovered the biggest and meanest looking Rottweiler he had ever seen. But, just like she had said, the dog just lay there on the carpet, watching the repairman go about his business.

But the whole time he was there, the parrot drove him nuts with his incessant cursing, yelling, and name-calling. Finally the repairman couldn't contain himself any longer and yelled: "Shut up already, stupid bird!"

To which the parrot replied: "Go get him, Brutus!"

Racist!

Once in a while one slips by.

The Latest Elvis Sighting

Sam

A lady took her Poodle to the parlor for a haircut. When she asked what it would cost, the girl behind the counter told her "$60."

The lady was outraged: "I only pay 50 bucks for my own haircut!"

"But you don't bite, do you?" the girl replied.

Jim woke up one morning to find a gorilla sitting on a branch on the tree in his backyard. He looked through the yellow pages and called a gorilla removal service.

"Is it a male or a female gorilla?" the removal service guy asked.

"I think it's a male," Jim replied.

"No problem! I'll be right there."

Half an hour later the service guy showed up with a stick, a pair of handcuffs, a shotgun, and a dog. He handed Jim the handcuffs and the shotgun and said: "I'm going to climb this tree and poke the gorilla with the stick until he falls. When he does, the trained dog will bite the gorilla's testicles off. The gorilla will then cross his hands to protect himself and allow you to put the handcuffs on."

"OK," Jim said, "But what do I do with the shotgun?"

"If I fall out of the tree before the gorilla, shoot the dog."

It was a boring Sunday afternoon in the jungle, so the elephants decided to challenge the ants to a game of soccer. The game was going well with the elephants beating the ants ten to nothing, when the ants gained possession of the ball. The ants' star player was dribbling the ball towards the elephants' goal when the elephants' left back came stampeding towards him.

The elephant stepped on the little ant, killing him instantly. The referee blew his whistle, stopped the game, and gave the elephant the red card.

"Oh, my God! They've killed Kenny!" the other ant players screamed.

"What the hell do you think you're doing? Do you call that sportsmanship, killing another player?" the referee asked the distraught elephant.

The elephant cried: "I didn't mean to kill him! I was just trying to trip him!"

During the height of the cold war, the Americans and the Russians realized that if they continued their arms race, they were going to blow up the whole planet.

They arranged a top secret summit, where it was decided to settle the whole dispute with one dog fight. They agreed to give each other 5 years to breed the two most powerful fighting dogs ever.

The winning dog's country would be entitled to dominate the world. The losing side would have to submit and lay down its arms.

The Russians searched their vast country to find the meanest, most vicious Doberman and Rottweiler bitches and bred them with the biggest, most dangerous Siberian wolves.

They selected only the biggest and strongest puppy from each litter and fed it a diet of steroids and trained them to be lethal attack dogs. After five years of fierce breeding, Russia had managed to create the biggest, most vicious dog the world had ever seen.

Finally Russia and America met in Switzerland to let their dogs fight for world domination. Although its cage had 4-inch-thick reinforced steel-bars, everyone was afraid to even go near the Russian monster-dog.

When the Russians saw the American dog, they burst into laughter. America had sent a weird looking 9-foot-long Dachshund! The Russian breeders felt a little sorry for the Dachshund, because they knew it didn't have the slightest chance to last even 10 seconds against Russia's killer.

When the bell announced the beginning of the fight, the Russian dog leaped out of its cage, snarled, and charged the American Dachshund.

The Dachshund slowly waddled out of its cage towards the Russian dog. But just when the Russian champion looked like it was going to bite the Dachshund's neck, the Dachshund opened its mouth and swallowed the Russian dog with one bite. The Russian monster was gone!

The Russian politicians, shaking their heads in disbelief, walked over to the cheering Americans and said: "We don't understand how this could have happened. We had our best breeders working for five years with the meanest Doberman and Rottweiler bitches in the world and the biggest, meanest Siberian wolves!"

"That's nothing," an American replied. "We had our best plastic surgeons working for five years to make an alligator look like a Dachshund."

He's been gaining weight ever since he quit licking himself.

A New York businessman drove his car into a ditch in the middle of nowhere, somewhere in rural Pennsylvania.

Luckily, an Amish farmer came to help with his big strong horse named Abe.

He hitched Abe up to the car and said: "Pull, Esra, pull!"

Abe didn't move.

Then the farmer yelled: "Pull, Jacob, pull!"

Abe didn't respond.

Once more the farmer hollered: "Pull, Shilo, pull!"

Nothing.

Then the farmer said: "Pull, Abe, pull!"

And the horse easily dragged the car out of the ditch.

The New Yorker was most appreciative but couldn't help wondering about the names.

"Why did you call your horse by the wrong name three times?" he asked the Amish farmer.

The farmer replied: "Abe is blind. And if he thought he was the only one pulling, he wouldn't even try."

A man tried to sell a dog to his neighbor.

"This dog can talk," he said, "and he could be yours for only five dollars!"

The neighbor said: "What do I look like? An idiot? There ain't no such thing as a talking dog."

Suddenly the dog looked up with tears in his eyes and pleaded: "Please buy me, Sir! This man is cruel. He never gives me enough to eat, he never takes me for a walk, and he never bathes me! Before he kidnapped me, I used to be a famous trick dog in Europe. I performed on TV and before the Royal Family of England."

"Wow!" said the neighbor, "That mutt really can talk! Why would you want to sell him for five lousy bucks?"

"Because I'm getting tired of all his lies."

A three-legged dog walked into a saloon in the Old West. He limped over to the bar, ordered a drink, turned around, looked at the crowd, and announced: "I'm looking for the man who shot my paw."

Top Ten Things Television Teaches Us About Pets

1. Doggie schools have a 100% failure rate.

2. If someone finds a dog or a cat, they don't want it at first, then fall in love with it, keep it for 15 minutes, and then find it a loving home with a big back yard.

3. Dogs know how to turn on the TV and understand everything that's being said. In fact all pets are smarter than the people who own them.

4. Pets never shed or have accidents on the carpet.

5. All pet mice or snakes will escape at least once and be found by a woman standing on a chair, screaming.

6. Every pet will eventually run away from home because of hurt feelings.

7. Pets don't need any attention. And you don't have to feed them for months. They are perfectly happy just lying on the floor next to you, being part of the scenery.

8. Your cat will have a litter of 10, and within 30 minutes every last one of the kittens will have found a good home somewhere.

9. Lost something? Whatever it is, it's probably in the dog house or the cat basket.

10. Your dog is a much better kisser than your wife. And at night your dog's back feels exactly like your wife's legs.

Quit asking him these stupid questions! He ain't no Lassie, we don't have a well, and we don't even know anyone named Timmy.

GASPIRTZ

This is my pet rock Willy. My mom says our landlord won't allow cats or dogs.

A man and his dog walked into a bar. As they sat down at the counter, the bartender told them, that no dogs were allowed. The dog looked up at the bartender and said: "I don't see any sign posted about dogs."

The bartender was shocked and yelled: "Hey! Your dog can talk! This is incredible! Your next beers are on me!"

Both, the man and the dog, thanked him and drank their free beers. When the man had to excuse himself to go to the bathroom, the bartender leaned over the bar and asked the dog: "Could you do me a favor? My friend across the street is never gonna believe I met a talking dog. He'll think I've lost my marbles! He works at the 7-11. Here are 20 bucks. Could you go over there and buy a newspaper? A talking dog is gonna blow his mind! In return all drinks for you and your owner are on me for the rest of the night. And you can even keep the change from the $20."

The dog agreed, picked up the $20 bill in his mouth, and walked out of the bar. When the man came out of the bathroom, he wondered where his dog was, so the bartender told him what had happened. "What?! My dog is out there, crossing a street all by himself? He's gonna get hit by a car!" the man screamed.

He stormed out the door to look for his dog. He ran across the street, into the 7-11 store, but his dog was nowhere to be found. He ran up and down the busy sidewalk, but there was no sight of his dog. Finally he got to a dark alley, and heard his dog moaning and panting from behind a dumpster. Fearing the worst, he looked behind the dumpster. There was his dog - humping a French Poodle.

Shocked, the man stared at his dog and yelled: "Rex, how could you? You've NEVER done anything like this before!"

Rex looked up at up at him and replied: "Frankly, I've never had a $20 bill before!"

We had to send the lizards back to the wholesaler to get the bugs out.

We've GOT to get a bigger apartment!

Fashion Show

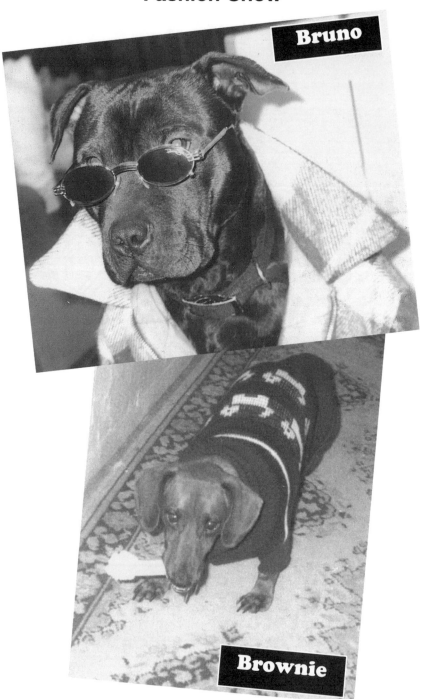

Bruno

Brownie

Mush

Andrea

Pssst! Hey, Mister!
When you're done over there...

More Amazing Animal Facts

In the last 4,000 years, no new animals have been domesticated.

The mouse is the most common mammal in the United States.

Dogs and bees can smell fear.

The horn of a rhinoceros is made of compacted hair.

All the swans in England are property of the Queen. Messing with them is considered a serious offense.

More people are killed annually by donkeys than die in plane crashes.

Some people say the fingerprints of koala bears are so similar to human finger prints, that they could be confused at a crime scene.

It is physically impossible for a pig to look up into the sky.

Did you know that an ostrich's eye is twice as big as its brain?

Shrimps' hearts are in their heads.

At 188 decibels, the whistle of the blue whale is the loudest sound produced by any animal.

Hummingbirds lay only 2 eggs during their entire lifetime.

Starfish don't have brains.

If you place a tiny amount of liquor on a scorpion, it will instantly go mad and sting itself to death.

Dragonflies can fly at speeds up to 30 miles per hour.

Did you know that ants don't sleep?

Sharks seem to be the only animals that never get sick. They are immune to every known disease, including cancer.

GASPIRTZ

A guy walked into a bar and asked: "Does anyone here own that big pitbull outside?"

"Yeah, I do!" a mean looking biker replied, standing up. "You wanna make something of it?"

"I think my chihuahua just killed him."

"What the hell are you talking about?!" the biker uttered disbelievingly.

"How could your little runt kill my pitbull? My dog could swallow your dog with one bite!"

"Well, he tried. And my dog got stuck in your dog's throat."

◆◆◆

Three race horses were talking to each other before a tournament. One of them started to boast about his track record: "Out of my last 13 races, I've won 7."

Another horse said: "Well, in the last 29 races, I've won 21!"

"Not bad, but in the last 35 races, I've one 27!" said another, flicking his tail proudly.

Suddenly a greyhound dog, who had been quietly sitting in a corner of the barn, walked over to the horses and said: "I don't mean to brag, but I've won 78 out of my last 80 races!"

The horses were totally shocked! "Wow!" exclaimed one of them after a hushed silence, "A talking dog!"

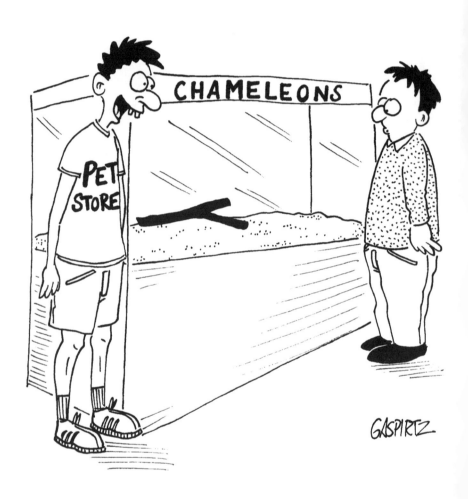

Which one do you want?

Good news is, you're not allergic to your cat. Bad news is, you're allergic to your veterinarian.

Merry Christmas!

Princesa

Casey

Top Ten Things You Don't Do With Your Pet In Public

1. Let your dog lick your feet.

2. Sing Barney songs to your cat.

3. Ask your pet what it would like for lunch in a squeaky high-pitched voice.

4. Talk to your cat about your relationship.

5. Bark at your dog and then look at his face to see if you actually said something in dog language.

6. Make loud bodily noises and laugh at the funny look on your dog's face.

7. Put off reading the paper because your pet is sleeping on it.

8. Give your little dog a bath and then hold it up in front of the mirror to show it how pretty it is.

9. Instead of cleaning up the mess, let your dog lick it up.

10. Give Aunt Wilma's casserole to your dog.

That means he likes you.

**My name is Bowser and
I'm a... I'm a... bad dog.**

GASPIRTZ

At a MENSA meeting, three men were arguing over who had the smartest dog. The first one, a math teacher, said his dog understood geometry.

The dog was named *Pie*. He told *Pie* to go to the blackboard and draw a square, a circle, and a triangle. *Pie* walked up to the blackboard, picked up a piece of chalk with his mouth, stood on his hind legs, and drew all three shapes perfectly.

The second man, an engineer, said he thought his dog was smarter. He told his dog *Calculus* to fetch a dozen cookies, bring them back and divide them into four piles of three. He did.

The third man, a chemist, said that was good, but he felt his dog was even better. The dog, named *Measure,* was told to get a carton of milk and pour five ounces into a six ounce glass. No sooner said than done.

All three men agreed that their dogs were unbelievably smart. A fourth man, a postal worker, who had been listening to the conversation, said: "That's nothing. My dog *Coffee Break* is the smartest!"

Then he told his dog: "Show these guys what you can do!"

Coffee Break went over and ate the cookies, drank the milk, "had his way" with the other three dogs, claimed he injured his back, filed for Workmans' Compensation, and then went home on sick leave.

Old McDonald's answering machine.

Gone With The Wind

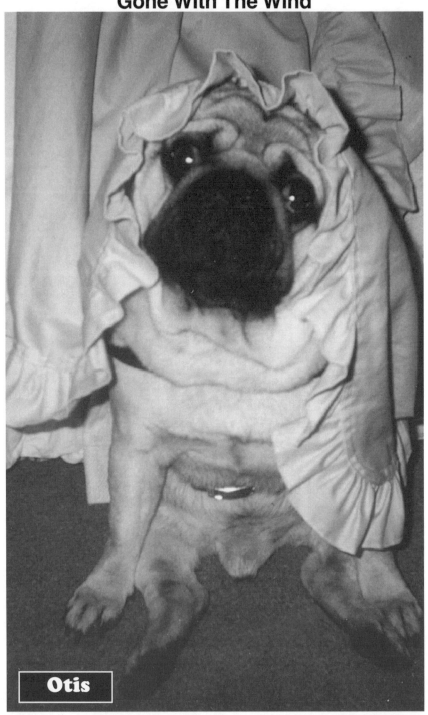

Otis

About the Author

Oliver Gaspirtz was born November 20, 1970, in Aachen, West Germany. Armed with a pencil and a Bachelor's Degree in English Literature he immigrated to the United States in 1993, where he married his wife Debbie.

He worked for a small weekly newspaper in Manhattan as art director and cartoonist, until his first book, *The Truth About Cinderella*, was published in December of 1993. He has been working as a freelance cartoonist ever since.

His award-winning cartoons frequently appear in many newspapers and magazines, including the *Saturday Evening Post, American Legion, SUN, The National Times, The Medical Post, Physician, Hippocrates, Nutrition & Health Review, Funny Times, The Comedy Magazine, Stand-Up Comedy, American Police Beat, Police, The Australian Police Journal,* England's *Punch,* and Germany's *Eulenspiegel.*

In Europe, his cartoons are being distributed by *Deike Press*, one of Germany's largest press services, and by the agency *PR Service Scherlinzky.*

His work can also be seen in over 20 major cartoon exhibits around the world, including exhibitions in Germany, Belgium, Italy, Poland, Lithuania, Iran, Japan, and the United States. The International Museum of Cartoon Art in Boca Raton, The Okhotsk Museum of Cartoon Art in Japan, The Cartoon Art Museum in San Francisco, The Ludwig Forum (Museum of Modern Art) in Aachen, Germany, and the Museum of Contemporary Art in Tehran, Iran, are just a few of the many museums that have added his work to their collection.

Gaspirtz is a member of the National Cartoonists Society, the Comic Art Professionals Society, and he is the New York representative of the Australian Cartoonists' Group.

Visit Oliver Gaspirtz on the Internet at: www.pethumor.com or send him e-mail at: oliver@pethumor.com

Also available from Lincoln-Herndon Press:

Grandpa's Rib-Ticklers and Knee-Slappers*	$ 8.95
Josh Billings - America's Phunniest Phellow*	$ 7.95
Davy Crockett - Legendary Frontier Hero	$ 7.95
Cowbody Life on the Sidetrack	$ 7.95
A Treasury of Science Jokes	$ 9.95
The Great American Liar - Tall Tales	$ 9.95
The Cowboy Humor of A. H. Lewis	$ 9.95
The Fat Mascot - 22 Funny Baseball Stories and More	$ 7.95
A Treasury of Farm and Ranch Humor	$ 10.95
Mr. Dooley - We Need Him Now!	$ 8.95
A Treasury of Military Humor	$ 10.95
Here's Charley Weaver, Mamma and Mt. Idy	$ 9.95
A Treasury of Hunting and Fishing Humor	$ 10.95
A Treasury of Senior Humor	$ 10.95
A Treasury of Medical Humor	$ 10.95
A Treasury of Husband and Wife Humor	$ 10.95
A Treasury of Religious Humor	$ 10.95
A Treasury of Farm Woman's Humor	$ 12.95
A Treasury of Office Humor	$ 10.95
A Treasury of Cocktail Humor	$ 10.95
A Treasury of Business Humor	$ 12.95
A Treasury of Mom, Pop & Kid's Humor	$ 12.95
The Humorous Musings of a School Principal	$ 12.95
A Treasury of Police Humor	$ 12.95
A Treasury of Veterinary Humor	$ 12.95
A Treasury of Musical Humor	$ 12.95
A Treasury of Victorious Women's Humor	$ 12.95

*Available in hardback

The humor in these books will delight you, brighten your conversation, make your life more fun, and healthier, because "Laughter is the Best Medicine."

Order From:
Lincoln-Herndon Press, Inc.
818 South Dirksen Parkway
Springfield, Illinois 62703
Tel: (217) 522-2732   Fax: (217) 544-8738
http://www.lincolnherndon.com